MIGHTY BEARS

D1303822

Photographs by: Big Stock Photo (bear up tree, p. 3); **Emerald City Images/Minden Pictures** (p. 20); **Getty Images** (polar bear, cover; p. 1; polar bear cub, p. 3; grizzly bear, Kodiak bear, p. 6; p. 8–9; pp. 12–13; p. 18; bear with cubs, pp. 20–21; black bear, p. 22); **Ingram Image Library** (polar bear, p. 7); **iStockphoto.com** ©Alexander Hafemann (Vatnajokull Glacier Iceland background, pp. 2–3); ©Erlend Kvalsvik (polar bear, p. 2); **Photodisc** (sky, cover; bear cub, black bear, p. 3; bear cub, p. 4; black bear, p. 7); **Photolibrary** (p. 5, sloth bear, p. 6; sun bear, polar bear, pp. 22–23); **Photo New Zealand** Mauritius Images/Thorsten Milse (pp. 10–11); **Alamy** (bear catching seal, pp. 18–19); **Tranz/Corbis** (brown bear, cover; pp. 14–17; Kodiak bear, p. 22)

All illustrations and other photographs © Weldon Owen Education Inc.

Author: Lynette Evans
Designer: Amy Lam
Photo Researcher: Jamshed Mistry

Published in the United States by
Scholastic Inc.
557 Broadway
New York, New York 10012
www.scholastic.com

Printed in China by Toppan Leefung

ISBN 13: 978-0-545-13896-3
ISBN 10: 0-545-13896-5

Library of Congress Cataloging-in-Publication Data

Evans, Lynette.
  Mighty bears / by Lynette Evans.

A CIP catalog record for this book is available from the Library of Congress.

15 16 17 18
10 9 8 7 6 5

CONTENTS

 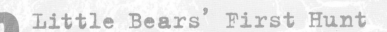

What do most bears eat?
How do bears learn to hunt?

Real bears are not like teddy bears at all. Real bears can be **DANGEROUS!** They are **predators**.

Bears are powerful animals.
Most are big and strong.
Some are good hunters.

Some bears eat meat.
Others eat mostly plants.
Look at the chart to
compare what bears eat.

Sloth bear

Kodiak bear

Grizzly bear

Grizzly bear	Sloth bear	Kodiak bear	Polar bear	Black bear
Length: 6–8 feet from head to tail	**Length:** 4¾–6 feet from head to tail	**Length:** 6–9 feet from head to tail	**Length:** 7–11 feet from head to tail	**Length:** 4½–6¾ feet from head to tail
Weight: about 250–900 pounds	**Weight:** about 120–420 pounds	**Weight:** about 240–1,720 pounds	**Weight:** about 880–1,750 pounds	**Weight:** about 200–600 pounds
Territory: North America	**Territory:** India and Sri Lanka	**Territory:** islands off Alaska	**Territory:** the Arctic, Alaska, Greenland, and northern Canada	**Territory:** North America, including Mexico
Habitat: mountains; in and around lakes, rivers, and streams	**Habitat:** grasslands, forests	**Habitat:** tundra; mountain and forest areas	**Habitat:** shoreline, sea ice, open water	**Habitat:** forests
Diet: elk, deer, moose, fish, plants, berries	**Diet:** ants, termites, fruits, honey, eggs	**Diet:** salmon, some plants	**Diet:** ringed seals, seal pups; walruses, fish, birds	**Diet:** fruits, nuts, pinecones, honey, fish, ants, fawns
Special feature: Many grizzly bears hunt at streams during salmon season to feast on the fish.	**Special feature:** The sloth bear has long claws for tearing open ant and termite nests. It sucks the insects out.	**Special feature:** This is the biggest of all brown bears. It is also called the Alaskan brown bear.	**Special feature:** Polar bears have black skin and see-through hairs to help trap heat and stay warm.	**Special feature:** Black bears come in different colors! They can be brown, white, blue-black or black.

Black bear

Polar bear

LITTLE BEARS' FIRST HUNT

It is spring. The little bear cubs and their mother are up. It has been a long winter in the **den**.

Spring means it is time to hunt.

The little cubs are young polar bears.
Polar bears live in the cold Arctic.
In spring, a mother bear is hungry.
She has not had food all winter.

She did not hunt. She stayed in her den to feed her cubs. Now she looks for food. Her cubs follow her.

Arctic

Sometimes a little cub gets a ride!

Polar bear cubs are born in snow dens during the winter. Young bear cubs drink their mother's milk.

The mother bear
walks to the sea.
That is where seals live.
Seals are **prey**
for polar bears.

A mother polar bear
lives off her body fat in
winter. She needs to eat
and fatten up in spring.

PREY

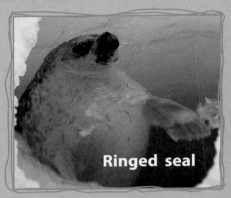

Ringed seal

Seals are a polar bear's favorite meal. Seals have their babies in the spring. The seal pups live in snow-covered **lairs** on the ice. Polar bears hunt for the pups in their lairs.

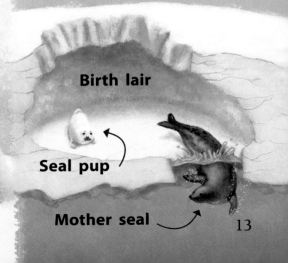

Birth lair

Seal pup

Mother seal

13

At last, the bears get to the sea.
The mother bear sniffs.
The little cubs watch.
Then the cubs sniff too.
The bears smell seals.

Bears have a good sense of smell. Polar bears can smell seals up to three miles away!

The bears wait on the ice.
Their white fur is hard
to see in the snow.
It keeps them **camouflaged**.
That way, they may not
be seen by their prey.

Polar bears sometimes
hide their black nose
with their paws – or
even a block of ice!

DANGER!

Arctic wolves are also hard to see in snow. A mother polar bear must keep her cubs safe from wolves.

Arctic wolf

The mother bear eats the seal meat.
Then she cleans her white fur.
The mother eats so that she
can make milk to feed her cubs.
The cubs drink her milk.
They will grow bigger
and stronger.

One day, the little cubs will be mighty hunters too.

21

BIG, BUT FAST!

Kodiak bears are the biggest of the brown bears. They stand on their hind legs to look around. They can run as fast as 35 miles per hour.

SMALLEST

Sun bears might be small, but they have mighty long claws for tree climbing. They use their 10-inch-long tongue to lick up termites.

CLIMBING CHAMP

American black bears climb trees to escape danger. Trees are also a good place for a back scratch!

BUSY BEAR FACTS

Run, swim, climb — can bears do it all?

ALL-STAR ATHLETE

Polar bears are the biggest predators on land. They can run as fast as 25 miles per hour. They can jump over cracks in ice. They can swim far and dive underwater for as long as two minutes.

MEASURE AND COMPARE

Some bears are tall. Some other animals are taller. See how bears measure up.

Find the tallest bear. What height is it?

Find the tallest animal. What height is it?

Polar bear

Horse

Sun bear

Dog

Person

Kodiak bear

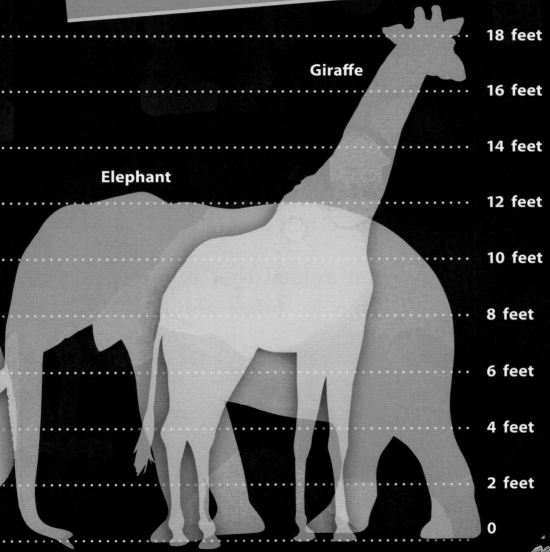

Measure a friend. Compare his or her height to the animals on the graph. Which is closest?

18 feet

Giraffe

16 feet

14 feet

Elephant

12 feet

10 feet

8 feet

6 feet

4 feet

2 feet

0

25

camouflage – to hide or blend in with surroundings

den – a home of a wild animal, such as a bear or a wolf

lair – a place where a wild animal, such as a seal pup, rests or sleeps

predator – an animal that hunts and eats other animals

prey – an animal that is hunted and eaten by other animals

American black bear in a den

Young bears stay close to their mothers. They watch what she does. From her, they learn how to take care of themselves. Find out more.

Book

Wendorff, Anne.
Bear Cubs
(Blastoff!).
Scholastic Inc., 2009

Web Site

www.kids.nationalgeographic.com/Animals/
CreatureFeature/Polar-bear

Polar bear